Lessons Learned as a Nazarite
By Zachary James

*Copyright © 2025 by Adonais Nazarite Training LLC.
All rights reserved. No part of this work may be
reproduced, stored in a retrieval system or transmitted
in any form by any means, electronic, mechanical,
photocopying, recording, or otherwise, without written
permission of the publisher.*

ISBN: 979-8-9985143-1-9

Dedication: 3
Dear reader, ... 5
I. So it Begins… 7
II. Childish Thinking 21
III. Growth 29
IV. Seek to Know Him 38
V. A Deep Revelation 45
VI. Trance 55
VII. Who Makes the Grass Grow? 62
VIII. Image 70
IX. Measuring Rod 76
X. Life's Meaning 84
XI. Protector or Destroyer 90
XII. How Much Do I Believe? 96
About the Author 106
Works Cited 107

Dedication:

I want to dedicate this book first and foremost to God. If it wasn't for You watching over and guiding me, I don't even want to imagine where I could be. Thank you! Blessed are You O'Lord my God!

Secondly, to my children. May God continue to shine His light upon each of you. Renewing each of your minds and giving each of you a new fresh heart which has been circumcised and deeply engraved with His perfect Word. Know that I love each of you, more than any of you can possibly understand at this present time.

Dear reader,

The journey of becoming a Nazir is one I would not recommend for any believer, Jew or Gentile. The whole process forced me to grow in ways I didn't even know were possible. I had to learn to look at God in ways that I will try to put into words, but let's face it, how can a finite being ever fully describe or understand the only One who is infinite.

This is my only warning to you, the reader. The stories and lessons contained in these pages may challenge your view of the God of Israel. May His sovereign Name reign forever! My hope is that we can have an open dialog so each of us can grow deeper in our relationship with the Lord Most High.

Unless otherwise stated, all Biblical references will be from the Complete Jewish Bible (CJB). It's fine if you, the reader, don't have one. Follow along using your own preferred translation.

May Adonai bless you and keep you!
May Adonai make His face shine on you and show you His favor!
May Adonai lift up His face toward you and give you peace!

                                        Numbers 6:24-26

I. So it Begins…

"I have taken you from the ends of the earth, summoned you from its most distant parts and said to you, 'You are my servant' — I have chosen you, not rejected you" -Isaiah 41:9

My teenage years lasted from 1998-2005. As a teenager I was mostly filled with rage, hate and/or apathy towards everyone, regardless of who they were. I even had a sick running joke with my friends that we were neither racist nor sexist, we were just simply an "ist," we hated everyone equally. At the time, I would've laughed in the face of anyone who told me "You're going to believe in and trust God Almighty," the same God whom I loved to hate. So, imagine my surprise in 2010; after following Him for about 4 years, I had the strangest and strongest desire to take on the Nazarite Vow wash over me. To be honest, I was extremely hesitant to comply with a seemingly ridiculous idea, initially thinking of this "vow" as something for ancient people. I really didn't understand why I had a desire to take it on, nor did I have the faintest idea on how to complete it. When I sought the counsel of my first Rabbi, he gave me a simple yet self-evident suggestion, "If the desire is as strong as you say, then look into what it would take to even perform the Nazarite Vow." In the simplicity of his answer, he was right. I needed God's guidance to show me how to perform this vow of His, because like an explorer walking into an unknown forest, I truly had no clue of the adventure that lay ahead of me or the challenges that awaited.

The Nazir Vow is a very unique type of commitment in the Bible with its governing laws being held in Numbers chapter 6. Any other mentions are in passing, mostly of those who are examples of it being lived out. The whole purpose of the vow is to set oneself apart more than the typical believers in God. In Hebrew, the word "Nazir(נזיר)" can be translated to mean "consecrated," "separated," or in some cases, as "monk." Traditionally this vow is used when an individual wants to grow into a deeper understanding or relationship with God, or when wanting to make a deeper, and not so average, offering. A Nazarite should not be confused with a Nazarene. Nazarenes are those from Nazareth, or the early followers of Yeshua of Nazareth. Whereas a Nazarite are those who are actively under, or have successfully completed, a Nazir Vow.

I will freely admit, I am not a big fan of most traditions, and I don't usually give them much more than a passing thought. Personally, I find many traditions too restrictive or arbitrary, plus I have a bad habit of forgetting to perform them on a regular basis. The whole idea of celebrating any tradition has never sat well with me, who cares if something has been done for thousands of years? If the whole reason it's started is from some arbitrary reason, then why should I participate? So, if the Nazir Vow was truly what God wanted of me, then I needed to understand the *how* and *why* behind the whole practice. One statement God made towards Moses stood out, "**Tell the people of Isra'el, 'When either a man or a woman makes a special kind of vow, the vow of a nazir, consecrating himself to ADONAI,'**" then "**Throughout the time of his being a *nazir* he is holy for ADONAI**" (*Numbers 6:2,8*). This statement made it clear I would change, but at the time, I just didn't understand how different I would eventually become.

    Even though the Torah (1st five books of the Bible) is for today and for those who believe in Yeshua, I started my knowledge seeking quest with the Talmud, which is a collection of different Rabbis debating their interpretations of the Torah. The Mishnah (a portion of the Talmud) had a lot of helpful suggestions, even though it gave strange regulations for a Nazir. Restrictions like a ban on combing through hair with a brush; some reasoned it would partially rip hair out. I could, however, use my fingers as a make-shift comb. This made no sense, why could I use my fingers but not a brush?

Either way the result would be the same, I could just as easily accidentally yank out hair follicles with my fingers as I could with a brush. It also states elsewhere that I can wash my hair with shampoo but not with dirt (*dirt was a way to wash one's hair in the ancient world*). As any husband can testify to, there's almost always a gross hairy blob monster left behind on the wall or in the shower drain after his wife has finished bathing. Why then was washing of the hair not forbidden if hair can be pulled out during the washing process? Those, and some other traditions of the Nazarite Vow found in the Mishnah, really came across as arbitrary and borderline absurd.

One thing I found interesting was *Studies in the Weekly Parashah* by Yehuda Nachshonai. Nachshonai basically makes a comparison of how a Nazir can be either a sinner or saint and no one will be able to really tell the difference, because they both must perform the same actions. He stressed that the Nazir needs to rise to his goal through abstinence, not make abstinence the goal. This understanding really sets the pace of what it means to be a Nazir, or any kind of covenant really. Regardless of whether it's nazir, fasting, or marriage. The goal should not be the vow itself but learning to enjoy the journey while on it, which inevitably allows all of us the ability to grow into a

deeper relationship with and understanding of
ADONAI IF we so chose to.

    Swan diving into the Bible proved to be really fruitful as well. First, for those who don't know how to interpret Scripture, here are some very simplistic and basic rules.

    A. The Torah (The 5 Books of Moses) is more of a guidebook than anything else. It has too many stories for it to be a full-blown law book, and there are also too many laws for it to be a simple story book. Which is why, when going through the Bible, consider the Torah as complete and the rest just expand on what is taught in it.

    B. The phrase "Scripture interprets scripture," is a great way of pointing out the beautiful synergy of the Bible. The phrase means that multiple sections of the Bible will talk about similar situations, and each section is needed to give a fuller and deeper understanding of the overarching concept as a whole; it gives practical applications of what to do or not to do. Each smaller story helps paint the bigger picture, and each of those stories then helps contribute to an even bigger painting of God's overall beautiful message to mankind.

    C. We also need to understand the context of who, what, when, where and why each book of scripture was written. A Jewish mindset and understanding is different from a Greek one. All scripture was penned by Israelites, except for the two written by Luke, who was more than likely an acolyte of Jewish believers at the time. Even still, languages have difficulty translating from one to another, which makes it easy to lose the full meanings of cultural idioms and poetry when out of context of the original language and mindset. Meaning, if we don't understand these points of reference, how can we understand the difference between a "good eye" or an "evil eye," of which Yeshua brings up in Matthew 6:22-23. Or the "Seat of Moses," as referred to in Matthew 23:2-3. John H. Walton's approach of, "For us, but not to us," is a great way to remind the contemporary reader of the need to keep these timeless lessons in its cultural context.

There are five basic tasks anyone wanting to be a Nazir must perform:

    1. Do not drink alcohol of any kind: "**he is to abstain from wine and other intoxicating liquor**" (*Numbers 6:3a*).

    2. Do not consume vinegar: "**he is not to drink vinegar from either source**" (*Numbers 6:3b*).

3. Do not eat any part of the grape or its vine: "**he is not to drink grape juice, and he is not to eat grapes or raisins. As long as he remains a *nazir* he is to eat nothing derived from the grapevine, not even the grape-skins or the seeds**" (*Numbers 6:3c-4*).

4. Do not shave your head during their entire consecration and let your hair grow long: "**Throughout the period of his vow as a *nazir*, he is not to shave his head. Until the end of the time for which he has consecrated himself to *ADONAI* he is to be holy: he is to let the hair on his head grow long**" (*Numbers 6:5*).

5. Do not come near dead bodies, no matter who it belonged to: "**Throughout the period for which he has consecrated himself to *ADONAI*, he is not to approach a corpse**" (*Numbers 6:6*). In verses 7-8 we find out that even if the corpse belongs to a direct family member, they're not allowed to go near them. Most of the laws of a Nazir are pretty self-evident as to why they're there. This one, however, has taken me a long time to fully understand and wrap my head around its meaning and purpose. I will dedicate a whole chapter to it later. Continuing on, verses 9-12 details what happens if a person up and dies next to a Nazir. Quite the simplest of tasks, right?

Outside of Numbers chapter 6, Nazir's are not spoken of much. No blatant timeframes or stipulations on what the vow must be or for how long. According to the Talmud, if no timeframe is indicated, then the vow is assumed to be a minimum 30-day period. The Talmud also stipulates that the vow only counts while in Israel proper. If the vow is made outside of Israel, then the Nazir must restart the whole vow once they step foot inside the country's borders. Regardless, God makes it clear, a Nazir is different from both prophets and priests when He says "'**I raised up some of your sons to be prophets, other young men of yours to be n'zirim. People of Isra'el! Isn't that true?**' asks *ADONAI*. '**But you gave the *n'zirim* wine to drink and ordered the prophets, "Don't prophecy!"**'" (*Amos 2:11-12*). With that, only one person in all of scripture is blatantly called a Nazir, all others are either implied or is a traditionally held belief by Jews, Christians, or both.

- Samson (*Tribe of Dan - Nazir from birth till death*). "**For indeed you will conceive and bear a son. No razor is to touch his head, because the child will be a *nazir* for God from the womb. Moreover, he will begin to rescue Isra'el from the power of the P'lishtim**" (*Judges 13:5*).
- Samuel (*Tribe of Ephraim - Nazir from birth till death*), was not

allowed to cut his hair, "**Then she took a vow; she said, "***ADONAI-Tzva'ot*****, if you will notice how humiliated your servant is, if you will remember me and not forget your servant but will give your servant a male child, then I will give him to *ADONAI* for as long as he lives; and no razor will ever come on his head**" (*1 Samuel 1:11*).
- Absalom (*Tribe of Judah - Nazir for a set time period.*) "**At the end of forty years, Avshalom said to the king, "Please let me go to Hevron and fulfill the vow I made to *ADONAI*. Your servant made a vow while I was staying at G'shur in Aram to the effect that if *ADONAI* would bring me back to Yerushalayim, then I would serve *ADONAI*"** (*2 Samuel 15:7-8*).

Absalom is an interesting case to say the least, but like Samson's story, one does not have to be perfect to be a nazir. I do find myself going back and forth if I agree with the Jewish held belief of him being a Nazir. One thing is for certain, God will take care of those who blatantly disobey

Him. "Avshalom happened to meet some of David's servants. Avshalom was riding his mule, and as the mule walked under the thick branches of a big terebinth tree, his head got caught in the terebinth, so that he was left hanging between earth and sky, as the mule went on from under him" (*2 Samuel 18:9*).

- John the Immerser (*Tribe of Levi - Nazir from birth till death*), was not allowed to drink alcohol, "**for he will be great in the sight of *ADONAI*. He is never to drink wine or other liquor, and he will be filled with the *Ruach HaKodesh* even from his mother's womb**" (*Luke 1:15*).
- Paul of Tarsus (*Tribe of Benjamin - Nazir for an unspecified time period/task*), "**Sha'ul remained for some time, then said good-bye to the brothers and sailed off to Syria, after having his hair cut short in Cenchrea, because he had taken a vow; with him were Priscilla and Aquila**" (*Acts 18:18*).

- The strangest of which are found in the book of Acts. There are four found there but none of their names or tribes are given. "**So do what we tell you. We have four men who are under a vow. Take them with you, be purified with them, and pay the expenses connected with having their heads shaved. Then everyone will know that there is nothing to these rumors which they have heard about you; but that, on the contrary, you yourself stay in line and keep the *Torah*"** (*Acts 21:23-24*).

With all this knowledge now buzzing around in my head, I had to seriously pray for what was being asked of me. I knew I was not going to take a 'womb to tomb' kind of vow, and I didn't know if I had the faith to keep this vow till my death, which is why for my Nazarite vow, I started on June 3rd, 2011.

The ritualistic purity of being a Nazir was hard to maintain, as vinegar is a preservative used in a lot of American foods and condiments. This sucks for me because I love mustard, it is truly the best dipping sauce for fries, and don't even get me started on the orange deliciousness known only as Buffalo sauce. Vinegar is also a preservative used in salad dressings, canned soups, and most jarred foods. Frozen grapes on a hot summer day were one of my favorite treats growing up, even to this day. At one point my beard and hair grew so long that my employer wanted me to trim it all back; he said it was longer than what was allowable for males. Thankfully, through the Mercy of God, I was quickly shown a little thing called a "Religious Exemption" inside their employee handbook, which my employer had to abide by. Therefore, my hair grew longer. During the time of my vow, I received many funny looks, and some people questioned if the whole process was just for show. Some people even threatened to cut my hair against my will, and I got ridiculed more times than I can remember. The longer my vow went on, the more I realized how many people didn't fully understand what I was called to do. I'm ok with their lack of understanding, it was not meant for them. The whole point was for me to grow.

  On April 15, 2016, I finished my vow's task and finally shaved my head. How did I cleanse with no Temple? I had no choice but to improvise. I purchased flour and olive oil and mixed both with my shavings. I made sure to cleanse and anoint a grill, where I placed all the contents on wood. Then burned it all together. Because of the Messiah's sacrifice, the only thing I did not burn was an animal. The ashes created were collected up and dumped in the middle of nowhere, away from any city.

Now as I write this book in 2025, looking back at the challenge, I'll say this: I'm thankful that God asked me to take it on. Maybe the sages were right, once one has successfully completed a Nazarite Vow, then that individual will always hold the title of 'Nazir.' The key word there is successfully. I also now understand and agree with why most sages in the Talmud discourage people from ever taking on the Nazir vow. It's no simple task, and it should not be taken lightly.

II. Childish Thinking

"When I was a child, I spoke like a child, thought like a child, argued like a child; now that I have become a man, I have finished with childish ways" -1 Corinthians 13:11

I didn't grow up believing in or loving God. Put bluntly, I hated the version of Him sold to me by the world. I'll freely admit, I was angry and stupid. I never knew who God actually was because of my own self-absorption, I was only taught how to blame Him for all the troubles in my life. Consequently, this also allowed me to be convinced it was all God's fault, or at least, that He was the chief conspirator. How could someone so great, powerful, and loving allow the hardships I went through as a little boy? Why would a little boy deserve to go through what I did? At the time, I was convinced of false narratives like:

"It's God's fault I was the product of a drunken affair. God caused my birthfather to question the legitimacy of my relation to him. God forced him to choose drugs and a different woman over his own blood."

Except, it wasn't God's fault. He didn't start the cascading dominos that caused me to be the black sheep of the family or make me question my own value everyday afterwards. I was made through the decisions and actions of two broken individuals trying to figure out how to live their own lives. It takes a different kind of thinking to realize that our own parents are the results of their own shortcomings and choices, just as their parents were before them. It's through this realization that we can come to understand we're not so different from the people before or around us.

When I was 7 years old, a babysitter molested me then repeatedly jumped on my older, non-verbal, disabled sister. He cracked her head against the bar of an old metal chair, splitting her scalp wide open and spewing blood everywhere. Though they were very terrible, God didn't cause any of those actions either, a lost child who thought there were no consequences for his actions did.

When I self-harmed and did drugs as a teenager, I did it all because I was upset with my current situation and I desperately wanted to feel something other than anger. My childish and selfish way of thinking stopped me from venting in a healthy manner, which prevented my escape from the clutches of Self-Hatred. This reality truly made me think that my birthfather didn't care for me, and it caused the shattering realization that my mother couldn't always protect me from the dangers of this world. It wasn't until I was much older did, I realize that God <u>did allow</u> those events, but He <u>didn't cause</u> them to take place. So then, why would a loving, all powerful God allow such travesties? It's simple, He has a high and utmost respect for our free will. There are spirits in this world, other than God, who want to stunt the growth of humanity and harm them to get back at God. These spirits hate God, and since they can't hurt God, they attack His most loved possession, which is us. By causing us pain and leading us away from Him, they in turn cause God pain. It's the only thing they can do to Him.

    Nothing I went through as a child was ever easy or always fair, but this doesn't mean God wasn't there with me in the midst of my troubles. As an infant, I woke up needing to nurse right as my mother, in her brokenness, was getting ready to blow out the furnace pilot light to end the life of her little family of 4. This simple act of nursing pushed away my mother's darkest thoughts; this small act pushed my mother back into the arms of God. She was not perfect after that night, but it caused her to realize her need for Him every day.

    A problem we all eventually face is telling God how to do his job. This idea is both arrogant and juvenile, as if somehow, we could do a better job with our narrow and constipated viewpoints. How often do we stop and consider the bigger picture or the long-term effects of our actions and decisions? But instead, we think we're automatically right and everyone else is either wrong or stupid. Many people, instead of trying to learn a lesson from these incidents, would rather have not gone through trauma as a child. But how else do we learn to empathize with others? It's one thing to hear about a travesty, but it's a completely different level of understanding to live through one. On top of all that, one person's "trauma" is another's Monday-Night show. Unfortunately, we live in a broken world with broken people who choose to will their brokenness and demons as an inheritance to the younger generations who are still learning how to live, thus perpetuating the same cycles over, and over, and over again.

When my high school girlfriend ended up pregnant, my initial statement was quite literally, "You're welcome to leave, but leave the kid behind. I want it." I know the pain of having an absent father, so I couldn't bring myself to intentionally cause the same pain. All my suffering taught me to empathize, and it built in me a desire to help others through the same pain I suffered. But even then, my ex and I were still just kids ourselves who needed to heal from the issues we went through in our own childhoods. To assume there are cookie cutter lives is laughable.

Yitzchok Kirzner has a beautiful way of describing the difference of mindsets in his book The Art of Jewish Prayer. So good in fact, I'm going to let him describe it.

"Imagine that you are a 3-year-old child and you want a piece of cake. In fact, not only do you want a piece of cake, but you want to eat the whole cake! Your considerations as a 3-year-old are, "If I want cake, then I am entitled to it, and I must have it." From the viewpoint of a young child, the major function of parents is to gratify the child's wishes. When they don't the child feels angry and deprived. Now imagine yourself in the place of the parent of the child who wants the cake. You happen to know that if the child were to eat the cake, he would get sick, or would lose his appetite for nutritious food for the rest of the day. From the parent's perspective, how would you feel declining the child's requests? How great is the difference between the child's feelings and that of the parent in the same situation! ... Now imagine a third scenario. You see a cadre of men stabbing a person with knives. They proceed to knock the victim unconscious, saw open his chest and suction out his blood. How do you feel upon witnessing such a scene? When you are told that you are witnessing a man undergoing open-heart surgery, how do your feelings change? One of the fundamental differences between how children and adults view the world is that children filter the world primarily through their emotions whereas adults can rely more on their intellect to make sense of their experiences." (Kirzner, pages 3 & 4)

I like Rabbi Kirzner's description; it reminds me of an interaction I had with my oldest daughter when she was about one and a half years old. My ex, our daughter, a group of friends and I had gathered at a popular fast-food joint for lunch. To say that I love spicy food is an understatement; I grew up in Colorado and did a lot of traveling to New Mexico. Hatch Green chilis are the best, and Serranos go in everything. Back to my point, while we sat there, I had Buffalo sauce to go with my waffle cut fries. My daughter, being so small, loved to dip her fries in everything ketchup. On this particular day, she tried to dip her fry in daddy's Buffalo sauce. I tried twice to tell her no, and I pushed her hand away each time, but she was not having it. Annoyed at me stopping her, she tried a third time, at which point I no longer cared, so I pushed the spicy orange goodness towards her… Enter the blood curdling screams the moment her taste buds understood what was now on them. She couldn't get the buffalo sauce away from her fast enough. I tried to give her a drink and a fry with just ketchup, but she refused to touch anything from my hand and stared at me with a deep look of betrayal etched onto her face. Isn't this how we all treat God? We reach for something over and over again because we think we need the drugs or the sexual partner, so God warns us not to make stupid decisions, but when we finally get what we want, we turn around and blame God for something we did to ourselves, and we act like He betrayed us.

It's through these childish mindsets that we yell and scream at God about how He sucks at His job, while we simultaneously think we're right in our viewpoint. We try to convince others of our justification to condemn God, saying "He needs to be better at His occupation," only to elicit the rightful response of, "Who are you? What qualifies you to run the universe and all that is in it?" Regardless if the pain is because of our own folly or the pitfalls of others choices, we're not God. We <u>DO NOT</u> get to decide how the world works, we only decide how we respond to life's storms.

III. Growth

"Their delight is in *ADONAI*'s *Torah*; on his *Torah* they meditate day and night. They are like trees planted by streams — they bear their fruit in season, their leaves never wither, everything they do succeeds" -Psalm 1:2-3

Charles Theadore "Chili" Davis, a U.S. Major League Baseball player from the 1980's and 1990's, once stated, "Growing old is mandatory, growing up is optional." Most people take this sentiment to mean one's ability or desire to mature as they age. I would, consequently, venture a guess that the vast majority of people only consider the physical world implications of this statement and not the spiritual. But isn't our spiritual health more important than our physical health? What good will this body be after we're dead?

A lot of new believers think they're now out of Egypt (sin) and are in the promised land, but that isn't how the story of Exodus plays out. The ancient Israelites wandered the desert for 40 years after exiting Egypt; they had to learn to grow and live with God before they could go up to the land flowing with milk and honey. They complained the whole time, like a bunch of kids in the back seat asking, "Are we there yet?" They also questioned and challenged God at every step, even though He only wanted the Israelites to go straight to the promised land. So, they hemmed and hawed and dragged their feet instead of just going. Isn't it the same when raising kids? *I don't want to clean my room. I don't want to come inside. I don't want to finish my meal.* Siblings bicker about how they didn't get their favorite cup, or how they don't want to share their toys. Kids will test a parent's patience in every way possible, as do all of God's children test His patience while they stumble around trying to figure out how to crawl and walk in spirit with Him. God is patient with us and will correct our paths, just like any good parent, even when we do not want Him to, which is why King Solomon says, **"My son, don't despise ADONAI's discipline or resent his reproof; for ADONAI corrects those he loves like a father who delights in his son"** (*Proverbs 3:11-12*). This is also why Paul says that **"...all discipline, while it is happening, does indeed seem painful, not enjoyable; but for those who have been trained by it, it later produces its peaceful fruit, which is righteousness"** (*Hebrews 12:11*).

    I'm no different, I fell down often as a young believer. Once in 2007, when I was very clearly falling short as a father and husband, my ex-wife and I got into a bad verbal argument. The funny thing is, I don't even remember what the argument was about, not that it matters anymore. It was late at night when she left for work, bawling her eyes out because of something stupid I said, which left me with the task of putting the kids to bed. At the time I only had two, so no big deal. My oldest got into her bed as I placed her new baby brother into his crib. As soon as I put him in, he was out like a light, no fighting, no fussing. I turned to look at my oldest and the same thing. I distinctly remember thinking to myself, "That's weird." What small kid doesn't argue about going to bed? Shrugging it off, I silently left the room. As soon as I shut the bedroom door, an unseen voice, as clear as day, whispered behind me. "Read," is all it angrily growled through clenched teeth. "Ummm... What?" "Read," the mysterious voice, just as angrily, uttered again.

Confused, I just walked to the living room and plopped down onto our couch. Again, I heard the voice, "Read," was all it said. As I was trying to figure out what on Earth this voice was trying to communicate, my eyes fixed on the Bible set on the table directly in front of me. "Read!" I heard it again, but this time it was a little louder. Leaving the Bible on the table, I used one hand to flip it open. It landed on the opening page of Proverbs, "Read!" My body started trembling, as I had no clue what was about to happen. The moment I let the first set of words cross my eyes, I felt this presence like I had never experienced before drop on top of me, covering my whole body. It penetrated deep into the core of my bones. The pressure didn't feel evil, quite the opposite in fact. It was, however, VERY angry at me.

As I read, every time I came to a part where it talked about a stupid or foolish man, His voice raged in my ears, "<u>This is what you are doing!</u>" Every time Proverbs talked about a wise or righteous man, His voice would still rage, "<u>This is what I want you to do!</u>" Louder and louder, He bellowed in my ears about my poor behavior, and each time I could feel His presence getting angrier and angrier.

At about halfway through Proverbs, I dropped the open book into my lap and tried leaning back to cry, instead I was pushed forward, "You're not done," He told me. The tears were wiped away from my eyes by His unseen hand, so I continued to read. Over and over again I was told how I needed to act versus how I was acting. When I finally finished the book, I had to literally throw the Bible away from me as I collapsed sideways onto the couch, weeping bitterly from my own humiliation. I could feel His presence all around me, and I somehow knew one simple fact, "I'm going to die right here on my couch if God's presence presses in on me just a smidgen more." A judgement was about to be decided depending on what my next choice of words were.

After a while, the only words I could even muster were simply, "I'm sorry, I didn't know, I'm sorry." Immediately, His whole presence changed from anger and frustration to that of love and compassion. God grabbed my left arm to sit me up, and I felt his other arm draped across my shoulders. Very gently He whispered into my ear, "I know you've been screwing up, but I also know you can do better, so do better." For a while after, I couldn't even stop myself from crying because of my own shame. Even when my ex-wife returned home from work, I couldn't bring myself to look at her because of the shame of my actions. She started to cry again because she thought I was still mad at her. It wasn't until the next day when I could tell her what had transpired the previous night, because I needed to process this unusual experience for me to finally find the words.

I wish I could say that was the last time I ever screwed up, but it wasn't. I was a toddler, and this is the expected behavior of a toddler. The falling down and the scraping of knees, wrists, or the occasional bump on the head is all part of the growing process. The problem arises when we choose to stay at that level of maturity. We need to continue to learn and grow and seek to understand the God of the Universe and the 'how's' and 'why's' of His ways. The best part? He's willing to show us His ways **IF** we ask!

God gladly uses the ancient Israelites as examples of both how to and how not to walk with Him. When they started out in Egypt (bondage), they had to cross the Red Sea (redemption) into Midian and finally end up in the Promised Land (full freedom). It's while they traveled through Midian that the Israelites learned how to walk with God. We each have to learn how to swallow our pride and come to terms with how little we actually know about God. The world gladly lies to all of us about so many things. It lies about how there is *no God, find your truth*, or *inner power is the only power*. Worst still, our prideful natures really don't want to accept the truth about who God actually is, which is why it's easier to believe these lies.

Just like the ancient Israelites, we each have nations (vices) in our lives that we need to conquer. We each need to heed the orders given by God, because "**ADONAI your God will expel those nations ahead of you little by little; you can't put an end to them all at once, or the wild animals will become too numerous for you. Nevertheless, ADONAI your God will give them over to you, sending one disaster after another upon them until they have been destroyed**" (*Deuteronomy 7:22-23*). God is the one destroying those nations before Israel. Too many of us think that we have to break our vices by our own strength, but we need to conquer them based on His strength. He will do it little by little so that we slowly learn to grow and trust Him more and more. Just like in my first time hearing His voice, it was a small step of Him correcting my path.

Why slowly, city by city? The biggest reason is the snowball effect. It's the small victories which give us the motivation to keep going, just like a small bit of snow rolling down the side of a mountain can cause a powerful avalanche. This slow process also allows us time to become accustomed with the new lifestyle we're still learning. This way, we can make sure to live every day in our new level of understanding, removing the clothes of our old understanding and desires, because God Himself has made us into a new nation (new creation) being built up by His strength and wisdom.

Why do we need time to adjust? You need time to adjust because "**[w]hen an unclean spirit comes out of a person, it travels through dry country seeking rest. On finding none, it says, 'I will return to the house I left.' When it arrives, it finds the house swept clean and put in order. Then it goes and takes seven other spirits more evil than itself, and they come and live there — so that in the end the person is worse off than he was before**" (*Luke 11:24-26*). Our old selfish desires will come back with a vengeance. Those times in our lives when the same thing happens to us over and over again. This is the reason. We need to learn to stop behaving in the way of our old nature and start walking in the way of our new lives. Learning to tell ourselves 'No' is not an easy process, especially with the world screaming at us to give in to every desire, and "You Only Live Once" (YOLO). Self-seeking pleasure is normal for the world, but as a new nation (new creation) we need to be more concerned and cognizant of God's perspective over everything. Just like how we slowly learned our old ways, we need to slowly learn a new way, a way which leads to life everlasting. My suggestion is to learn to walk with God and taste that His Word is good. This is why you should "**…rid yourselves of all malice, of all deceit, hypocrisy and envy, and of all the ways there are of speaking against people; and be like newborn babies, thirsty for the pure milk of the Word; so that by it, you may grow up into deliverance. For you have tasted that ADONAI is good**" (*1 Peter 2:1-3*).

IV. Seek to Know Him

"As for you, Shlomo my son, know the God of your father. Serve him wholeheartedly and with desire in your being; for *ADONAI* searches all hearts and understands all the inclinations of people's thoughts. If you seek him, he will let himself be found by you; but if you abandon him, he will reject you forever" -1 Chronicles 28:9

God is so amazing! In Exodus 33:1-6 God tells the people of Israel to go and take the Promised Land, saying He will hand all the current inhabitants over to the Israelites. The only catch? God will not be among them because He's angry with them and worried that He'll destroy them in His anger. Honestly, rightfully so, for the people had just made a golden calf. Leading by example, God takes a moment to calm down and consider what to do with the people of Israel. This means that in Exodus 33:3, God is showing us how to be angry. He's clearly taking a moment to calm down so that He doesn't act out of anger. He's literally displaying the kind of behavior He expects from us. God leading by example gives credence to the later verses like, **"You can be angry, but do not sin! Think about this as you lie in bed and calm down,"** and **"Be angry, but don't sin — don't let** the sun go down before you have dealt with the cause of your anger" (Psalms 4:5, and *Ephesians 4:26*).

Hold up, it gets better!

"**Now, please, if it is really the case that I have found favor in your sight, show me your ways; so that I will understand you and continue finding favor in your sight....**" (*Exodus 33:13a*). Did you catch that? Moses is asking God to show him His ways. Not only does Moses want to know God's way of doing things, but he wants to understand them as well. Moses desires to have a deeply intimate relationship with God, the kind one gets from a healthy parent-child relationship. Moses could've just as easily whined and pleaded with God, but he didn't. Instead, Moses chose to seek and understand the situation because he sees that God is extremely angry, terribly offended, and deeply hurt by the Israelites actions of rebellion. Yes, the people are sorrowful for their actions and are trying to repent, but they didn't grasp the bigger picture. What does Moses do in this situation? He seeks to understand God's bigger plan and asks Him to continue to be the God of these people. Curiously, in verse 17 we find God's response of, "**...'I will also do what you have asked me to do, because you have found favor in my sight, _and I know you by name_**'" (*Exodus 33:17, emphasis added*). What amazing displays of leadership! God shows us how to be angry by taking a moment to breathe, and Moses shows us how to have a relationship with God by desiring to understand His perspective.

Let's take this one step further by applying this understanding to the scariest verses in the whole Bible: "**Once the owner of the house has gotten up and shut the door. You will stand outside, knocking at the door and saying, 'Lord! Open up for us!' But he will answer, 'I don't know you or where you come from!' Then you will say, 'We ate and drank with you! you taught in our streets!' and he will tell you, 'I don't know where you're from. Get away from me, all you workers of wickedness!'**" (*Luke 13:25-27*). I can understand the fear people have from these verses. Who really wants to be rejected by an all loving and good God? Especially when we think we're being a "good" person. God wants us to follow Him and His ways of doing things, but not for the sake of our own reputation. God knows the secret inclinations of all human hearts. He'll know if we're doing acts of charity because we're being coerced, bribed, afraid of the court of public opinion, or because we want to help build His kingdom. God knows who wants Him for the sake of Him being Him and those who only want Him because of what He can do for them. Of course, He's not impressed by the latter.

Back in Exodus, the people do things in God's name but don't want to know His reasoning, which is why they openly rebelled when they thought He wasn't watching, or He was taking too long to perform an action. Moses, on the other hand, wanted to see God's face and know Him intimately. Much like a young child sitting on their parent's lap studying their face, Moses wanted to understand why God does what He does. God, showing His character, acknowledges Moses' request. This is what set Moses apart from the rest of the people. This same mindset is what set Kings David and Josiah apart, as well as the prophets, like Samuel, Isaiah, Jeremiah, John the Immerser, Peter, and Paul. It's what sets any "hero" of the bible apart from the average individual following God.

    When we seek to know, understand and follow His plan, God is truly pleased because we seek to have a relationship with Him. Think about it, if the only time any person sought to talk with their spouse was on the Sabbath for an hour or two every week, how successful would their marriages be? What if we only talked with them on the holidays? What if we never sat with our spouses to try and understand their anger, sorrow, or joy? How could we still be considered married? We would be strangers! The point is, God wants to hear from us! He cares! And He's willing to listen to each of us about all our troubles because He actively seeks to know us. Why don't we reciprocate that for Him? He has blatantly shown each of us how much He loves us, so why don't we show Him the same? What's the point of having a relationship with a mindless drone, one who only acts based on pre-approved programing? Following God's commands should not be about wanting a "Get-out-of-Hell" pass. You should follow God because of how overwhelming your love for Him is, so much so, that it's nearly impossible to imagine a life without Him. A life where it's an act of joy to simply do what He asks because He is the one asking.

Consider the structure of the Jewish declaration of faith, commonly referred to as the Sh'ma: "**Hear O Israel, the LORD our God, the LORD is one. Love *ADONAI* your God with all your heart and with all your soul and with all your strength**" (*Deuteronomy 6:4-5, Tree of Life Version*). In order to fully love God, we must first learn to do so with all of our hearts. In other words, circumcise our hearts like Abraham did in Genesis 15:6. Then we can learn to love with all of our soul, much like the sons of Korah in Psalm 42:2-5. Only afterwards can we fully trust God with all of our strength and resources, similar to what Rabbi Paul mentioned in 1 Corinthians 13:3. The Sh'ma is structured to be the path through the ever-darkening forest of the world, guiding those who are willing to brave the journey to the Promised Land.

"*But it's impossible to know God.*" BULL! That idea is nothing more than cowardice and ignorance. Such a statement only means you don't want to set aside time every day to get to know Him; it means you'd rather make up excuses and say it's hard or inconvenient. No kidding. There isn't a relationship which is always easy or convenient. All relationships take work, sacrifice, and compromises. It takes learning to swallow your pride and admitting that your actions were messed up. It takes realizing that we're not perfect, nor are we always right. There is hope though, and it's this beautiful motivation called love. "**Love is patient and kind, not jealous, not boastful, not proud, rude or selfish, not easily angered, and it keeps no record of wrongs. Love does not gloat over other people's sins but takes its delight in the truth. Love always bears up, always trusts, always hopes, always endures**" (*1 Corinthians 13:4-7*). This is what God does to each of us every time we make a mistake and come back to Him with a humble heart. Don't believe me? Go read Genesis 3:21-22, Jeremiah 30, Ezekiel 3:18-21 or Luke 15:11-32 to see some examples. There are more of course, but those are just the tip of the iceberg. God Himself paved the road for us to return back to Him IF we so choose to.

My suggestion? Be like the biblical heroes and seek the Face of God! Learn to love God with everything you have, just as He has taken the time to love us with all He has. In the end, "**…every**

knee will bow and every tongue will swear" (*Isaiah 45:23*) that *ADONAI* is God, but will the knees bow out of brute force or loving respect?

V. A Deep Revelation

"It is to us, however, that God has revealed these things. How? Through the Spirit. For the Spirit probes all things, even the profoundest depths of God. For who knows the inner workings of a person except the person's own spirit inside him? So too no one knows the inner workings of God except God's Spirit" -1 Corinthians 2:10-11

One of the deepest realizations of life comes when we fully realize how loving God actually is. Sadly, this epiphany sometimes comes from the darkest points of our lives. Mine was no different.

I'll freely admit it; I was no prince charming in my first marriage. The only excuse I have is that I didn't know better because I was a selfish jerk. Regardless, the end of 2015 was when we had our final falling out. In October of that year, I was reminded of a dream I had back in the Summer of 2011, one that told me I was going to get a divorce. A dream that I, for the longest time, didn't want to believe. A dream that I couldn't get any relief from, as I had it every night for a solid month. Eventually, I started seeing it every time I closed my eyes, I couldn't get it out of my head. I feared it would eventually shatter my mind, so I begged God, "Either take this dream from me, or let it shatter my mind and make me forever known as a babbling fool!" Nothing, I didn't see it again… that is, until October of 2015, when I saw it once more.

During the Hanukkah week of 2015, my children and I watched as their mother packed her things and moved out. Every single night I tried to convince her to celebrate with us, but to no avail. December 12, 2015, was the final night for her in our little apartment. Over the next week I heard nothing from her, not even a call to ask about the kids or the dog. I was a wreck that first week of our separation; I barely ate or slept. With only a brave face for my kids, I held myself together as best as I could; although, I don't think I did a very good job.

At the time, I was working security for some building in the Rocky Mountains. Wednesday morning it snowed a decent amount and was still actively piling on when I took my father-mobile, also known as a minivan, and headed into my mediocre job. The morning road's killer combination of being exceptionally icy and snow packed always makes mountain driving that much more precarious. Such a good combo in fact, that the road went right, and my van went straight. I fell roughly 5 feet into a smooth, open field that was buried in fresh, powdery snow. After skipping like a rock on a pond, I came to a complete stop in the middle of the field. Thankfully, the only injury I sustained was a bruised ego. Praise God I didn't fall

200 feet sooner, or I would have submerged into a frigid thinly iced pond, and if I fell 200 feet later, then I would've gone into a rocky bend. In the end, the only damage to the minivan was scratched paint and very minor dents. Even though the tires were practically bald and had wires showing on the inside walls, they miraculously did not pop or flatten. After the crash, a coworker that I had came and picked me up, since I was only a few minutes from the job site. Even though a miracle had just transpired right in front of me, God didn't receive my attention.

    The following day, my favorite mentor went with me to a sketchy car dealership in the city because my van was still sitting in the middle of a field. The process took a while, but I was blessed with a newer car that day. Honestly, it was the nicest car I'd ever owned at that point in my life. It wasn't very roomy, but it definitely allowed me to transport all of my kids. According to my oldest, all cars need a name, so she dubbed it "Silver Fang." Did I stop and give thanks to God for such a blessing? You bet I didn't, all I could see was my own misery: "Self-pity! Party of one!" I did realize that the car was a blessing, but I, unfortunately, was still very blinded by my own crumbling life.

    Then came December 20th, 2015. It had been just over a week since the last time we spoke, and now here she was picking up all of the kids and our only dog. The lonely apartment was much emptier than I had expected, and it quickly became one of the hardest and most unforgettable nights of my life. For the first time in about 13 years, I went to a dark place that I was all too familiar with from my teenage years. A place where depression, self-loathing and self-harm each had their own fully furnished rooms. And on this terrible night, I was committed to becoming a permanent roommate of their house. I had a tub ready with warm water and a razor nearby for my trip down the street.

As I stepped toward the bathroom, I heard a small pleading whisper from behind me, "Worship Me!" *What?* I thought. At this point, I didn't want to worship God, I just wanted everything to stop hurting. I was a failure; my life was crumbling in front of me. Shame became my only friend, as I had failed at being a husband, son, father, and a man in general. *Worship Him? Pfft… Whatever! What could He possibly understand?* Again, He quietly whispered, "Read Psalms and Worship Me. What else do you have to lose?" He was right. I had just lost everything; I couldn't lose anything of higher value than what I had already lost. Besides, I was convinced that nothing was going to change, and that tonight was going to be my last night on Earth anyway, so why not.

I flipped open the Bible sitting on my desk and landed on Psalm 150; from there, I started reading it backwards. Nothing changed with the first chapter but then came chapter 149. **"Sing to *ADONAI* a new song, his praise in the assembly of the faithful. Let Isra'el rejoice in their maker, let Tziyon's children take joy in their king. Let them praise his name with dancing, make melody to him with tambourine and lyre; for *ADONAI* takes delight in his people..."** (149:1-4).

"THAT MEANS YOU!" God's voice spoke as clear as day. It was as if He, Himself, was standing right next to me. I froze trying to process what had just happened. His voice echoed in my mind as I began to stutter trying to continue reading Psalm 149. My eyes were looking at the page, yet I couldn't read the words; they had changed to a garbled mess and might as well have been Chinese, for how little I could understand them. I went back to the beginning of the chapter, and the same problem arose. I couldn't read a single letter on that page anymore, except for verse 4a, **"for *ADONAI* takes delight in his people."** Every time my eyes glanced at that phrase, an echoing of His voice reverberated in my ears, "That means you!"

Breaking like a dam, I couldn't hold it back anymore: streams of tears, an opened faucet of runny snot, and drool all poured from my face. A banshee screech fled from my crumbling body as I hit the floor. God's presence filled every square inch of my room. It was so thick and evident that I could even feel Him deep inside the core of every one of my bones. There I lay on the floor, letting out all of my pain before Him in deep, guttural moans and cries. There the Molder and Fashioner of the entire Universe sat with me in the bedroom of a rundown apartment. The One who established the very foundations of the Earth and set the boundaries of the seas. The only One who can loosen the belt of Orion and knows all of the ordinances in Heaven, yet He took the time to stitch me together in my mother's womb, knowing the exact number of hairs on my head. This same Supreme and Majestic Being was there with me in the midst of my grief and sorrow. He didn't care that I'd failed horribly and helped to ruin everything I'd come in contact with. He wanted to be right there in that room to comfort me and to make sure that I was cared for. He did all this for no other reason than because it was me. He loved me first, a nobody living on a wet rock in the middle of some obscure part of the Universe. He wanted to be there with me, at that moment, for no other reason than because of who He is.

     On that night I experienced one of the greatest characteristics of who God is. He IS love. He loves us more than any of us could even begin to comprehend. We fail and blatantly break His laws repeatedly, either arrogantly or ignorantly. We drag His Name through the mud, yet He still desires to be with each and every single one of us in spite of our shortcomings. He knows we're all stupid and imperfect, but He IS love. Even when we don't want to love ourselves or Him, He loves us. It's not because of what we have done or how important we think we are, He simply and unconditionally loves us.

Prior to that night, I never understood what love really was or how freeing true love can be. The world tells us that if someone loves us, then they'd do such and such, or if they truly loved us then, they wouldn't have done such and such. However, that thinking is pure stupidity and arrogant lies! The world is lying about what love is, for those are selfish and self-centered conditions. How can the world say something is love while simultaneously placing conditions on how to gain said "love?" That's not love, it's a contract! A robot only acts loving because it's programmed that way, it has no option but to follow its script. Love is not, and should never be treated as, just an arbitrary feeling of butterflies or an ooey gooey, mushy sensation of being pleased with someone simply because they make you feel happy or excited. Love is a choice which, I admit, is not always easy or fair. Letting go of an ego and swallowing pride takes practice.

God wasn't pleased with my behavior up to that point because I was being blatantly disrespectful, rude and willfully obstinate, yet He still chose to come and be with me in my brokenness. I didn't deserve His love nor attention, but that's what love does. I was clearly being, for a lack of better term, a shithead, not only to His Face, but to my ex-wife and children as well. He was trying to get my attention to help me and correct my path, but I ungratefully threw His compassion back at Him like a spoiled little brat.

One of the greatest acts of love is letting someone suffer the consequences of their own actions, even if it grieves our own heart. It allows both parties to live freely, because, by trying to control the actions of another person, it takes away their ability to learn, grow, and appreciate what they have. You need to allow them the freedom to choose love and to do so unconditionally. Plus, with being so neurotically controlling of another's behavior, do you ever really learn how to master your own?

"I may have the gift of prophecy, I may fathom all mysteries, know all things, have all faith enough to move mountains; but if I lack love, I am nothing. I may give away everything that I own, I may even hand over my body to be burned; but if I lack love, I gain nothing. Love is patient and kind, not jealous, not boastful, not proud, rude or selfish, not easily angered, and it keeps no record of wrongs. Love does not gloat over other people's sins but takes its delight in

the truth. Love always bears up, always trusts, always hopes, always endures" (*1 Corinthians 13:2-7*). It's this kind of love that God gives to everyone at every moment of every day. He was with me in that room because He loved me first. God wanted me for no other reason than because it was me. To those reading this, I know for a fact that God loves each and every single one of you in the same exact way. All we have to do is choose to learn how to love Him back. Accepting His love is the easy part. Learning to walk in it is something very different.

VI. Trance

"Listen to me, house of Yaʻakov, all who remain of the house of Israʼel: I have borne you from birth, carried you since the womb. Till your old age I will be the same — I will carry you until your hair is white. I have made you, and I will bear you; yes, I will carry and save you. To whom will you liken me and equate me? With whom will you compare me, as if we were similar?"
-Isaiah 46:3-5

    If you, the reader, haven't already guessed, I've had multiple supernatural encounters with the Lord Most High. Let me tell you about one event which left me incredibly amazed, awestruck, and dumbfounded. I lack the words to fully describe its impact on me, but what a night it was.

    In 2018 The Dead Sea Scrolls toured here in Denver, Colorado. I'd initially taken my kids to see it, but because I had to watch them, I wasn't able to truly appreciate the history being displayed. Doing the only rational thing, I came back later with a former acquaintance and not the little yahooligans. We both looked through all the artifacts and articles, and I must say, The Dead Sea Scrolls are truly a sight to behold. Near the end of the exhibit, there were two large blocks from the Western Wall.

People would walk up with tiny written prayers and place them into the crevices of the Wall because later they'd be placed into the actual Western Wall of Jerusalem.

When my eyes finally noticed these large blocks, I became transfixed. Immediately, I felt a strange pulsation slowly pulling me toward the massive stones. It took me a moment to realize the rhythm of the pulse, *Bump bump... Bump bump... Bump bump.* The closer I stepped, the louder and stronger the rhythmic heartbeat became, yet my eyes couldn't shift away from these stones. Slowly, the crowd's din was washed out by the pulsating beat. When I was close enough, I tried reaching out and touching one of them, but an invisible hand pushed my own hand down. "No," I heard whispered behind me. My fixation finally broke when the acquaintance of mine brushed past and brazenly touched the stones.

I spent the rest of the day trying to process the pulsating sensation I had experienced in the middle of that large crowd. Sleep left my eyes because every time I closed them; the heartbeat would ring in my ears and pulse through my body. Which made being ready for my night shift a fleeting dream.

Being the shift lead at the time, my work computer was in the main lobby with my front desk officer. From behind me, while I sat and miserably failed to focus, I heard my subordinate, a fellow brother in the Messiah, break the deafening silence. "What is going on with you? Why are you pulsating like a heartbeat?" I spun in my seat to look at him. "What do you mean?" I asked hesitantly.

"You're pulsing with energy; I can feel it. I'm just wondering why." I told him all of what transpired earlier that afternoon, and being truly amazed, we gave glory to God. However, needing to do my first walking patrol through the empty building, I got up and left him by himself.

As I walked past the first set of doors, I felt a fishing hook catch the inside of my cheek. The invisible line became tight and pulled me to the roof, my favorite place on the building. I've prayed there for many hours prior to this night. The southeast corner of the roof gave the best view of the landscape; from it you could see deep into a nearby valley and a large reservoir. If you look Northward, you can see a small mountain, and then in the next break, you get a clean view of multiple cities sparkling out in the distance. During the day you could see the mountains clothed in green trees and colorful flowers. At night, the stars shone like small pin pricks on a dark blanket, reminding one of how small we truly are. It really was the best place to be left alone for prayer. This is where the invisible hook pulled me to, and there I prayed to give God glory for His creative ability, the whole time I could hear the heartbeat ringing in my ears and pulsing through my body. I stood there for about 15-20 minutes praying before I stopped and walked away to try and finish my first patrol.

When I walked back into the building, the invisible hook latched on again and pulled me to the same spot. Once again, I stood praying and feeling the pulse. I don't know if I was ever called on my radio, not that it would have mattered, because the heartbeat was all I could hear. Another 15-20 minutes pass, and I tried again to finish my first patrol, but for a third time I was pulled back up to the roof for prayer.

I greatly cherish this memory, but not for the reason one would think. For the longest time, I've had this secret desire to sit in God's lap with my head against His chest so I could hear His heartbeat. The desire was born out of witnessing my own children do the same to me. All of them had at one time or another sat in my lap just to listen to my heartbeat. Oh, what beautiful memories of them! Every time any of them did it, they made me feel absolutely loved. Many times, I've secretly wondered if any of His creations had wanted the same thing I did. I wanted God to feel the same kinda love I'd felt from my own kids, but I always assumed I'd have to wait until I was on the other side. Never in a million years did I imagine being allowed to hear his heartbeat on this side of life.

Here lies the secret of that day, "**...when you pray, go into your room, close the door, and pray to your Father in secret. Your Father, who sees what is done in secret, will reward you**" (*Matthew 6:6*). God knows all of our secrets, even the ones we're afraid to utter for fear of ridicule. I wasn't granted this experience because I'm somehow special, I'm not! I'm just a nobody who knows a really special "Somebody." And this special Somebody knows and loves each and every single one of His children. I think I was granted this experience for two reasons. Firstly, while I wanted to hear God's heartbeat, what I honestly wanted more was for God to feel as loved as any other father who cares about his children. And secondly, I think God wanted me to know what it's like to sit in the lap of a loving Father, something I didn't really know growing up.

Honestly, it saddens me how the vast majority of people go through their day not considering God's perspective. Even worse still, those who claim to love Him but don't stop to consider His heart or feelings. These people treat Him like He's just some magic fairy, because they try to pull Him from their pocket whenever they want something, and as soon as they don't, to the trash heap He goes. Why? He truly asks very little of the human race, yet how many times do we all look at Him as a last resort. Don't get me wrong,

I'm in this boat as well, because I've done the same. We all, including myself, can do better.

VII. Who Makes the Grass Grow?

"*ADONAI* **said to Kayin, 'Why are you angry? Why so downcast? If you are doing what is good, shouldn't you hold your head high? And if you don't do what is good, sin is crouching at the door — it wants you, but you can rule over it'**" -Genesis 4:6-7

Throughout my walk I've struggled to keep in step with God, usually because of my own willful disobedience and blatant ignorance. It really isn't easy learning a new way of living. In 2007 I worked delivering newspapers to my local community, and one early morning during my route, I came across a soccer ball laying out by an apartment door. My first thought was, "Oh I can play soccer with the kids." Enter the now familiar small whisper from behind. "Leave it there, it's not yours." Three times He told me to leave the ball behind, but I didn't listen due to my own willful and selfish desires. The very next night, while I was preparing the papers for delivery, my van was broken into. The driver's side window was broken by the prying of a crowbar, which spilled glass all over the inside. I opened the side door to assess what was missing, and then the same soccer ball from the morning before came rolling into view, almost like it had been nudged to front and center. I knew immediately why my tools, car stereo, and breakfast had been stolen, they made me realize the need to quickly return the ball to where I took it from. What I should note is this: for a while after I was upset about my radio being taken, because, at the time of the theft, I had owned it for only a couple of weeks—two months tops. There are parts of me that really wish most of life's lessons were as easy to interpret as this particular morning. During my walk I have come to this simple realization, the more I try and aspire to be "good," the more I understand that I'm not good at all. It's during my times of stumbling that I've learned of my need for God's correction and forgiveness, usually because His thoughts and feelings were the last things I considered.

    I want to offer a piece of hope found starting in the garden in Eden. Adam, Eve, and the Serpent each received a different set of curses. The one that is interesting is when God tells the serpent, "...**You will crawl on your belly and eat dust as long as you live**" (*Genesis 3:14b*). Why would God curse the serpent with eating dust? Dust is literally everywhere. Few things in this world are more abundant than dust, so why curse the serpent with abundance? Why would self-sufficiency be a curse? It's almost as if God is telling the serpent, "There! You no longer have a reason to come near Me or anything that belongs to me again, now get away from Me and don't come back!" The serpent is self-sufficient so he will never have to be reliant on God for anything ever again. This gives a deeper level of understanding to all serpents found in scripture.

Case in point, the bronze serpent found in Numbers 21:4-9. Starting in verses 4 & 5 we see the people were grumbling about the detour and the food they had. They let their own narrow view of the current circumstance cloud what God was trying to do for them, which made their minds wander into the darkness of their own pity parties. Yes, physical snakes were sent to bite the people, but spiritual snakes were present as well, biting just as many, if not more. The snake from the Garden was there in the land of Edom, still whispering in the people's ears, causing them to grumble. He spoke lies like: *it was "good" in Egypt*, or *God has led you here to kill you*, or *yes, that fruit does look good and makes you wise like God*. It wasn't until after enough people had died from these snakes did, they finally choose to repent. And only after they repented, God instructed Moses to make a bronze serpent and attach it on a pole for everyone to see so that anyone who willingly looks upon this bronze snake can be healed supernaturally. In other words, God told Moses to hang a physical representation of the people's selfish desires, which is a curse, so that when the people willingly looked upon this representation and believed, it would heal them. Another way to look at it is this: we take our own selfish and fleshly desires and hang them on an execution stake so we may be healed. God provided a way for the people to be healed and saved from themselves because they weren't capable of saving themselves from their own stupid choices. Does this story sound familiar? "**Just as Moshe lifted up the serpent in the desert, so must the Son of Man be lifted up; so that everyone who trusts in him may have eternal life**" (*John 3:14-15*).

    Now let us go back to the story in Genesis. Right before she ate the fruit, Eve "...<u>saw that the tree was good for food</u>, that <u>it had a pleasing appearance</u> and that <u>the tree was desirable for making one wise</u>" (*Genesis 4:6a, emphasis added*). Adam was no better, he sat by and did nothing to stop this interaction, because Eve, "**… also gave some to her husband**, <u>who was with her</u>; **and he ate**" (*Genesis 3:6b, emphasis added*). Adam and Eve's desires got the better of them because they chose to allow their own fleshly desires to enter their hearts. Adam wouldn't admit to his own sin of adding to and not enforcing God's word, which let Eve be misled by the serpent. Adam even went as far as to blame God for him sinning (*Genesis 4:12a*). Similarly to the Israelites in Numbers, Adam and Eve mulled over their choices which allowed sin to enter their hearts, so then they both did stupid, just like me and every other single person across this planet.

This is where the beautiful part comes into play. The first two humans were afraid but eventually admitted to God what they had done. Because they were the first two to have ever sinned, they didn't know how to repent. God, seeing how those two acted out of ignorance and blatant lies, chose to forgive them. He, Himself, provided a covering for them. Yes, He had to kick them out of the garden for a time, but He needed to eradicate the source of destruction first so that He could eventually, both physically and spiritually, bring people back into the garden. The serpent, playing on both human ignorance and desires, was to be punished by being removed from God's presence indefinitely. When Adam and Eve leaned on God and willingly submitted to Him, He took away their sin, which takes the bronze serpent of Numbers to a much deeper level. God allowed the people to wallow in their sin and suffer the consequences until they chose to return because He then provided a way for them to come back. The only catch? People had to take those sinful desires and nail them onto a stake… *cough*cough* Cross *cough*cough*

Let's take this one step deeper. When God created us, He "**...formed a person from the dust of the ground and breathed into his nostrils the** breath of life, so that he became a living being" (*Genesis 2:7*). We also know that when people die, they "**...return to the ground — for [they] were taken out of it: [they] are dust, and [they] will return to dust**" (*Genesis 3:19, emphasis added*). There are other places that admit to man turning back into dust when we die (*Ecclesiastes 3:20, Job 4:19, 34:15*), so then this must mean the serpent is symbolically eating carnality, or our flesh. This is why I think Peter ominously warns us to "**Stay sober, stay alert! Your enemy, the Adversary, stalks about like a roaring lion looking for someone to devour**" (*1 Peter 5:8, emphasis added*). There are a couple of places where the enemies of God are licking the dust (*Psalm 72:9, Micah 7:17, Isaiah 49:23*) of the ground because they search for and eat the carnality of the world.

    One really cool thing about God is that He works in patterns; this is how we know He is ever unchanging. This unwillingness to change the methodology of His ways is how we know that He is always merciful, kind, just, and above all else Holy. I've done more than my fair share of idiocy, yet when I chose to come back to Him with a humble heart, God's always ready for me with open arms. This doesn't mean I don't suffer the consequences of my own mistakes; I do. I just know that when I am done acting like a fool, God will allow me to return. He's made a way for us all to come home, but each of us has to be willing to accept and choose this simple path. Choosing to follow God is not always easy or fun. It's this discipline of self-control which has taken me years to really master. Even to this day, I've repeatedly eaten big slices of humble pie, but it's made me come to this realization: life is not all about me and I don't always get my way. I've had to learn to take my own selfish desires and, even when I don't want to, put them on an execution stake.

The Messiah once said; "**God is spirit; and worshippers must worship him spiritually and truly**" (*John 4:24*). Given what was just pointed out about the flesh representing the serpent, I think Yeshua is just emphasizing what it means to place all of those desires on the execution stake. I also think He's answering the rhetorical questions of Elifaz in Job 4:17: "**Can a human be seen by God as righteous? Can a mortal be pure before his maker?**" We can't be seen as 'good' by God unless we approach Him in spirit and with honesty. We must actively put to death our old carnal nature so we can approach Him in spirit, like babies who are learning to walk, taking life day by day. Paul of Tarshish gives a detailed breakdown between the difference of both fleshly activities and spiritual ones in the book of Galatians 5:19-26. I highly recommend going and reading what he said for yourselves.

Being deep on the other side of my choice to submit, what I've gained astronomically outweighs whatever I've lost. I now have a joy which can't be stripped from me, but the biggest change is peace. I have peace. I have the peace of mind knowing that God is faithful to all of His promises. The only reason I keep going is because I have His strength and grace to hold me up. I'm not perfect by any stretch of the imagination, and I don't deserve to live, but by the grace of God am I a new creation. If you let Him, He'll "**...sprinkle clean water on you, and you will be clean; [He] will cleanse you from all your uncleanness and from all your idols. [He} will give you a new heart and put a new spirit inside you; [He] will take the stony heart out of your flesh and give you a heart of flesh. [He] will put [His] Spirit inside you and cause you to live by [His] laws...**" (*Ezekiel 36:25-27, emphasis added*). Letting God mold me and grow me into what He wants has truly been the best decision of my life.

VIII. Image

"Then God said, 'Let us make humankind in our image, in the likeness of ourselves; and let them rule over the fish in the sea, the birds in the air, the animals, and over all the earth, and over every crawling creature that crawls on the earth.' So God created humankind in his own image; in the image of God he created him: male and female he created them" -Genesis 1:26-27

  I've worked in security for most of my adult life, both armed and unarmed, Federal and private. Having also gone through a Police Academy, there's very little in security I haven't done. My occupation has allowed me to work with a wide variety of people, from a colorful array of backgrounds, and I can safely say, it's not always easy dealing with people, regardless of their socio-economic background status. Even harder still is learning to treat people with respect, especially when they're being blatantly disrespectful.
  <u>WARNING</u>: the stories I am about to describe all really happened, and I will not clean up anyone's language used towards me.
  The last couple of years I've been doing contract security across the Rocky Mountains' front range. One night, while working security at a gas

station in a kinda rough part of Denver, I came across three homeless people camped out on its property. As respectfully as I could; while maintaining good situational awareness, I simply asked them to pack up and move off property. One of the women in the group made an interesting comment towards me. "Thank you for talking with respect to us, not many people do. Why are you so respectful when all of the other security guards are fucking assholes." Without missing a beat, I said "Those who mock the poor, mock their maker. Those who reproach the poor, reproach their maker. The least you do unto them, you do unto me. So, if I am not willing to treat my God disrespectfully, why would I treat you disrespectfully since you bear His image." All three people just stopped and looked at me. The same woman finally broke the silence, "Wow! That's deep... where did you get that from?" Immediately I responded with, "Proverbs... It's a book in the Bible."

    I'll be the first to say, some people are easier to treat with dignity than others, especially when they're being respectful back or have an agreeable mindset. It's also easier in some situations versus others. During the time of the Black Lives Matter (BLM) riots, there was one angry woman who kept screaming "I want to tie you up so I can rape your daughters in front of you!" at me. It was one of the few times that I had difficulty maintaining composure. Once there was a male who kept saying racial slurs, and eventually he decided to spit blood at my feet (his injury was from another homeless male punching him). One of my subordinates had to tap me out because I almost lost it. He got me so angry that I threatened to empty a canister of pepper spray on him and then break my baton across his head. If I had done so, I would have rightfully gone to jail because of an unjustifiable use of force. In all situations, I try to remember that every person bears the image of God. I'm not always perfect at remembering this, but I do try.

   I also need to remember that I may be the only representative of God some people will see, which is why He says to never "**... take the name of the L**ORD **your God in vain [that is, irreverently, in false affirmations or in ways that impugn the character of God]; for the L**ORD **will not hold guiltless** *nor* **leave unpunished the one who takes His name in vain [disregarding its reverence and its power]**" (*Exodus 20:7, Amplified Bible*). When I chose to accept His free gift of mercy and grace, I took on carrying God's Name to the world; I became a representative of Him to the world. Right, wrong, or indifferent, I represent Him to the planet. The best way I can describe this is with government agencies or private corporation uniforms. Every uniform I've worn made me a representative of their agency or corporation. I worked with their authorization to enforce their rules and answer their questions from the public, as does every other person who wore the same uniform. Not everyone has the mental capacity or desire to distinguish between individuals wearing similar uniforms; therefore, if people have had negative interactions with those uniforms, then, to them, everyone in that uniform is automatically the same. Good luck changing their minds. No one hates a crooked cop more than a good one. No one hates a bad teacher more than a good one. The same is true of those who honestly and joyously bear the Name of God on their hearts.

Many so-called "Christians" and "Jews" have used the Bible in ways it was never meant to be used, because they lack understanding and they cherry pick verses to suit their own ideology. This makes them act either sexually, physically, fiscally, and/or emotionally abusive because of a lack of apathy towards their own destructive behavior. Too many people have been abused by those only "wearing" the Name of God, which is why hypocrites are a leading reason for many people to either leave communities or never enter them in the first place. This happens all because of people who didn't wear their uniform appropriately, and it gives God a repulsive image to the victims.

God requires His children to never "**...let grace and truth leave you — bind them around**

your neck; write them on the tablet of your heart. Then you will win favor and esteem in the sight of God and of people" (*Proverbs 3:4-5*). I can claim to believe in God all day long, but so what? Even demons believe in God, and it makes them tremble in fear. What good is my faith if I don't produce the fruit of my belief? God says there are standards on how I'm to treat everyone and standards on how I'm supposed to represent Him. If I don't follow those standards, am I being honest towards God or other people? I have His grace to cover me when I mess up, but if I don't get back up and try to live out His standard again, then I've truly failed and given up my belief in Him who redeemed me.

Being made in His image means that my identity is found in Him, and I don't get to change God's view of me to suit my own agenda. Similar to what Naomi tried to do when she said, "**'Don't call me Na'omi [pleasant],' she answered them; 'call me Marah [bitter], because *Shaddai* has made my life very bitter'**" (*Ruth 1:20*). I get it, she'd lost both her children and husband during their travels abroad. Despite this, she's never actually called 'Marah,' only two lines later the Book goes right back to calling her Naomi: "**This is how Na'omi returned...**" (*Ruth 1:22a*). In fact, the only times names are successfully changed is when God does it: Abram to Abraham, Sarai to Sarah, Jacob to

Israel, or Simon to Peter. Naomi wanted to change her identity because of her own feelings, but she didn't realize that God is the one who gives identities, regardless if we know our purpose or not.

    In David Stern's commentary section in the Complete Jewish Study Bible, he points out how the phrase 'to put my name on' is an idiom, with its meaning being to share one's own reputation. We can see this idiom when God says that "**...they are to put my name on the people of Isra'el, so that I will bless them**" (*Number 6:27, emphasis added*). God allows the people to have His reputation attached to them if they follow His commands. The people were to display and teach the other nations about God's nature. All the more reason to be cognizant if you chose to follow God, because people's perspective of Him is at stake.

IX. Measuring Rod

"Then the master summoned his servant and said, 'You wicked servant! I forgave you all that debt just because you begged me to do it. Shouldn't you have had pity on your fellow servant, just as I had pity on you?' And in anger his master turned him over to the jailers for punishment until he paid back everything he owed" -Matthew 18:32-34

Over the course of my life, I've had a hard time learning to forgive people, especially certain people who have helped to create pivotal memories. Eventually I learned to forgive the babysitter for what he did to me and my sister, my biological dad for leaving, and even his ex-girlfriend for beating me and locking me in a dark, windowless basement. I had nightmares well into my teenage years because of her actions towards me, but yes, I even forgave her. In my early 20's I had a phone call with a cousin from my biological father's side of the family. Through our long talk, she helped fill me in on what my father told his side of the family, which allowed me to finally forgive him.

The person I had the hardest time forgiving was my ex-wife. It took me literal years before I wouldn't be filled with rage at the mere mention of her name because of how badly she hurt me while we were still married and after the separation. She has repeatedly lied about me, repeatedly tried to manipulate me, and repeatedly threw things at me. In fact, she left the day before our oldest son's 9th birthday and said nothing to me for over a week, but then later chose to tell the courts how I left her and the kids. The worst offense being when she shut down a conversation, I was trying to have with my own grandmother Alida before she died. It was the one and only time in my entire life I was able to share and discuss the Bible or our faith with each other, the one time I was able to sit and openly try to understand my grandmother's Catholic viewpoint about God. My ex came in causing a scene to shut down our conversation saying, "A family event is no place for this conversation. Stop it!" There was never another opportunity for my grandma and I to speak so openly before she died. Oh, the anger I had for my ex was so intense afterwards. It took me over a decade just to forgive her for this single incident during our marriage. To put it into perspective, my grandmother died in the middle of 2011, the described event took place during the winter holidays of 2009, and it's currently 2025 at the writing of this book.

      Eventually I was reminded of Mathew 6:14-15: "**For if you forgive others their offenses, your heavenly Father will also forgive you; but if you do not forgive others their offenses, your**

heavenly Father will not forgive yours." Needless to say, I really didn't want to comply with this demand; I wanted justice for all the things she did to me. I may not have been a charming prince, but I didn't deserve half of the crap she did to me. The other half... well, I probably did, because I didn't always have a kind response for her snide and condescending remarks. One of the clearest signs of forgiveness is to want and pray for the success of someone who has done wrong to you, which can be a difficult task.

      The prophet Jonah's book is not a large one, yet in its small amount of pages, he is able to perfectly reflect a lot of people's stance on forgiveness. We want to live for and be used by God, but the moment we're told to do something we don't agree with, we turn away and run from the task. Think about it, Jonah struggled with extending God's mercy to a people he felt was undeserving of God's mercy. Jonah was delegated a task, but he didn't want to comply, so he ran from God and ended up drowning somewhere in the Mediterranean. Only for God to bring him back to life and have Jonah deliver the bad news of God's plan of destruction for the hedonistic gentile city of Nineveh. Afterwards, Jonah gets unreasonably angry because the city repented, allowing God to change His mind about their destruction. The last line of the book God says something to Jonah which really sums up His sentiment towards all peoples in general, "...**"You're concerned over the castor-bean plant, which cost you no effort; you didn't make it grow; it came up in a night and perished in a night. So shouldn't I be concerned about the great city of Ninveh, in which there are more than 120,000 people who don't know their right hand from their left — not to mention all the animals?"** (*Jonah 4:10-11*).

How is what I did to my ex any different than what Jonah did to Nineveh? I wanted God to dish out His justice towards her, because I didn't think she deserved His mercy because of what she had done to me. *Did He not see what she did to me? Or did He just not care?* Of course He saw, and yes, He cared about both of us. Our treatment of each other was not acceptable in His eyes. She failed as a wife, and I failed as a husband, but we both failed Him. God also still loves her just as much as He loves me. At the end of the day, she is still His daughter and still made in His image, nothing is going to stop Him from loving her with the full weight of the cosmos. She is also His problem to correct, not mine. My job is to follow what the Messiah said: **"For the way you judge others is how you will be judged — the measure with which you measure out will be used to measure to you"** (*Matthew 7:2*). Because I was not willing to show her grace, and I played tit for tat with her,

God had every reason to give the same exact treatment to me. Because He keeps His promises and won't let a single word of His fall short, what choice did I really have?

Please understand, God is not stupid. He could see I needed to grow and work through my ignorance so I could fully forgive my father. With my ex, I had to repeatedly go before Him and ask for help with my bitterness towards her; I needed His help to forgive her because I couldn't do it by myself. In both cases it took time, growth, effort on my part, and a WHOLE LOT of patience with me on God's part. He already understood and expected me to struggle with this process. I am no abnormality to humankind, and I am not special in any sense. Look at Jonah, Peter, King Saul and a plethora of other people in Scripture, some learned the power of forgiveness, while others did not.

I think learning to be forgiving towards others is one of the bigger lessons from Jonah. Nineveh was a large gentile city, and God forgave them even though they didn't deserve it. But really, does anyone deserve God's mercy? I don't know a single person who does. I most certainly don't, I definitely deserve death. Forgiveness, in of itself, is not always an easy lesson; it takes time to learn to let go of our claim to a perceived offense needing to be corrected. An old, grouchy coworker once said to me, "Justice is not merciful, nor is mercy just, but both are attributes of who God is." I think this is where a lot of us get hung up: our understanding of how the system works. You can rage and complain to God about needing to be vindicated, but the process of doing that chokes you out while letting the offender go on with life not really thinking about you. It continues to give them power over your life when they don't deserve such a pedestal. Honestly, what good would it have done me if I continued to hold onto and view myself as a worthless little boy whose dad didn't like him enough to stick around? The whole idea of refusing to forgive someone is like letting a constrictor snake squeeze the life out of you so it can eat you without a fight.

    I want to give one last warning to everyone reading this: If you come across someone who has wronged you in some way, and your first thought is to get justice or revenge for the offense, remember the warning given in Deuteronomy 7:6-11. The only reason any of us have any good in our lives is because of God's Mercy. It has nothing to do with who we are, because it was God who brought us out of Egypt (sin) and redeemed us for His Name's sake. It has nothing to do with what we could provide; instead, it has to do with our willingness to follow His path. In other words, how can anyone sit there and point fingers at another person when the accuser is no better than the person they're accusing? We want God to be merciful to us, yet many don't realize that another individual can't wrong anybody more than the many ways we've all wronged God. If we want God to be merciful to us, then we must be willing to be merciful to others. If the offender doesn't want to change their ways, fine! It's not your problem so you don't get to ridicule them, because it could've just as easily been you in the same dire need for somebody else's forgiveness. Which is why God says, "**Don't rejoice when your enemy falls; don't let your heart be glad when he stumbles. For *ADONAI* might see it, and it would displease him; he might withdraw his anger from your foe**" (*Proverbs 24:17-18*). He also says that "**…the Day of *ADONAI* is near for all nations; as you did, it will be done to you; your dealings will come back on your own head**" (*Obadiah 1:15*).

    Forgiveness is about healing. This does not mean you should continue to allow people to be abusive towards yourself, nor does it mean you get to be abusive back to them. You should separate yourself from the other person so that you can start healing the wound; you can't allow it to fester and putrefy, because it will eventually ooze and contaminate other aspects of your life. Unforgiveness and bitterness are worse than gangrene and leprosy combined. Please don't misunderstand me, I am NOT advocating abuse,

NO ONE deserves to suffer abuse, nor should they suffer in silence.

X. Life's Meaning

"Therefore fear *ADONAI*, and serve him truly and sincerely. Put away the gods your ancestors served beyond the [Euphrates]River and in Egypt, and serve *ADONAI*! If it seems bad to you to serve *ADONAI*, then choose today whom you are going to serve! Will it be the gods your ancestors served beyond the River? or the gods of the Emori, in whose land you are living? As for me and my household, we will serve *ADONAI*!" -Joshua 24:14-15

My life has not always been a belly full of laughter, nor has it always been a well of sorrow. I've had to learn to accept the easy parts along with the hard, which in of itself is hard since life can be crushing. No one would blame me if I hated life: I've been abandoned, molested, assaulted, and lied about by both strangers and people who claimed to love me. Yet I have also been loved, adopted, had children, and been a lamppost to people lost in darkness. So, which is life supposed to be? Joyful and carefree, or sorrowful and pain ridden?... Both... It's meant to be both.

I know that sounds cruel, but it's not. What's actually cruel is expecting life to be always easy and never being allowed to experience its downsides. I've had to learn to accept both parts of life to truly appreciate what it is, because if I never experience the bad parts, then how will I ever know when the good times come around? Remembering those good times is what has sustained me through life's difficult dilemmas. Unfortunately, there are too many people who claim the world needs to always be fair and comfortable, like somehow bubble wrapping everything and everyone will make life "good." Where's the freedom in that? There's no joy in being neurotically controlled. What's so "good" about not being allowed to experience life?

But doesn't God do the same by telling me how to live? No. He does, however, get to decide what is healthy and what is not, what is good and what is not, and how He's to be worshiped and how He's not to be. He IS the maker of ALL things in the Universe: to tell Him how to do His job is like the pot telling the potter how to make himself. The arrogance of such an idea! If I was a potter and I didn't like how my project was turning out, then I'd have the authority to smash the pot and start over. In this case, God actually is the potter, and He's trying to show each of us that there's a better way of life IF we want it. He's not going to force us to choose Him, even though the only thing of true value to God is our hearts.

But doesn't that mean God sends people to hell? NO! We send ourselves. God is literally giving us what we want; we don't have to listen to or follow Him. His perfect will is simply this: "**'I will engrave what is to be written on it,' says Adonai-Tzva'ot; 'and <u>I will remove the guilt of this land in one day</u>. When that time comes,' says Adonai-Tzva'ot, '<u>you will all invite each other to join you</u> under your vines and fig trees'"** (*Zechariah 3:9b-10, emphasis added*). God has no desire to watch anyone perish; He wants all of His human creations to be with Him. He's already provided a way to replace our filthy rags with flowing robes, but we arrogantly choose to live without Him. In His unconditional love for us, He won't make us spend eternity with someone we don't want to be with. That would be cruel!

Why doesn't God just show Himself and make it easier to know Him? He has! We're either too stupid or too arrogant to realize when God is trying to get our attention. Yes, I'm throwing myself into this mix. I was very dumb and arrogant when I was younger. The more I learned about who He actually is, the more I realized that I never understood who He was while I was a teenager. I was the stupid one, seeing as how God has called me stupid to my face. I'm okay with His analysis; He was right, I was being an idiot with a capital 'I.' What was I supposed to do? Argue with a Being who was right and could have snuffed me out in the blink of an eye? Not a wise idea my friend. It was my willfully ignorant and arrogant behavior which kept me from seeing who God really is and what He's doing in both my world and the world at large.

Paul puts it this way: "**I know what it is to be in want, and I know what it is to have more than enough — in everything and in every way I have learned the secret of being full and being hungry, of having abundance and being in need. I can do all things through him who gives me power**" (*Philippians 4:12-13*). Yet Soloman says it this way: "**Here is the final conclusion, now that you have heard everything: fear God, and keep his *mitzvot*; this is what being human is all about. For God will bring to judgment everything we do, including every secret, whether good or bad**" (*Ecclesiastes 12:13-14*). The older I get, the more I understand and agree with both of these men's assessments about life's meaning. If I hadn't been abandoned by my biological father, then hearing my oldest daughter's heartbeat for the first time wouldn't have taught me the full meaning of love at first sight... or love at first sound in that case. She's taught me what it means to have my beating heart walk around outside of my chest. Even now, while she's in full blown rebellion against God and blaming me and Him for things of which aren't our fault, she's still my beating heart.

But Zachary, my trauma wasn't my fault, and I didn't want to go through it. Yep, me too. I didn't ask to get molested by a babysitter. I didn't ask to get beaten and locked in a dark basement until my biological father came home. What I can do is turn all of my pain over to God and allow Him to heal me. Trust Him at His word when He says, **"Vengeance and payback are mine"** (*Deuteronomy 32:35a*). But at this point, I'd rather the people who harmed me come to know the God I know so that He can heal them from the scars they carry because their scars aren't their fault either. All I'm responsible for is how I choose to take my next step. Will I step towards God with an angry heart that wants to watch the world burn down around me, thus asking to be destroyed in the process, OR will I step towards God and lift up my broken heart asking Him to mend it, because I can't keep living in this world's pain, anger, and greed. I leave you with this final thought. **"So now, Isra'el, all that *ADONAI* your God asks from you is to fear *ADONAI* your God, follow all his ways, love him and serve *ADONAI* your God with all your heart and all your being; to obey, for your own good, the *mitzvot* and regulations of *ADONAI* which I am giving you today"** (*Deuteronomy 10:12-13*). As for me? I am going to follow the advice of Joshua 24:15-24. Since it will always rain at some point, regardless if I follow Him or not. I'm going to choose to enjoy life as it comes at me by dancing in the rain. I may look like a fool dancing, but at least I know I'm in good company and am where I belong. In the hand of Him who has made good on His promise of a fresh and newly circumcised heart.

XI. Protector or Destroyer

"They have lutes and lyres, drums and flutes, and wine at their parties; but they pay no attention to how *ADONAI* works and never look at what his hands have made. For such lack of knowledge my people go into exile; this is also why their respected men starve and their masses are parched from thirst" -Isaiah 5:13

While I was sitting quietly in service, the Rabbi told a story from the Midrash, which challenged the way I looked at my own livelihood. The story goes like this: *"A group of rabbis from the Sanhedrin go to various places in Israel to test the temperatures of the land. And in this one city, they didn't hear the clamor of children in the classrooms. They called the elders of the city out and said, 'show us the protectors of the city.' The elders paraded the soldiers out before these rabbis, in their full regalia with shining weapons and sturdy shields. And the rabbis looked at the elders and said, 'These are not the protectors, these are the destroyers. Where are the teachers?'"* (Roeh Israel). For several days after, I pondered this story for its full meaning.

In my line of work, I've had to become accustomed to violence and carrying the tools of a warrior. While I am always prepared to dish out justified violence, it doesn't mean I relish using it. While I do try to fully de-escalate every situation, not every circumstance can be resolved peacefully. I try to embrace the old adage of, "It's better to be a warrior in a garden than a gardener in a war." However, the story taught by the rabbi really shifted my viewpoint and made me think of many of my own work experiences—the ones where I could've easily enforced the rules and made circumstances harder for people just because of my own ego. Three of such situations come to mind.

    The first was while working security at a gas station in Denver. One night, as I patrolled around, I came across a homeless man about my age who was quietly sitting and reading the Bible by himself. God told me to buy this man a sandwich and water because complying with His command opened the door for me to talk with this U.S. Army Veteran. From speaking with him, I learned that this man's mom had just died. I also found out that he was estranged from his father, and his brother wanted nothing to do with him. He had also just been released from prison for a felony he admits was dumb of him to do. After talking with him off and on for the next couple of weeks, he eventually made the decision to head back to Kansas and make peace with his dad. I wonder what would've happened if instead of feeding this man, I told him to "kick rocks and beat it, there's no loitering on property."

In the middle of the night, during the winter of 2020, I was patrolling a parking garage in Lone Tree when I discovered a young male in gym shorts and a simple T-shirt. I was able to quickly conclude from his mannerism and repetitive fixed speech that this man was definitely mentally deficient. I quickly called medical for him, and it was later discovered that he had run away from a group home. He also became very agitated and distressed at even the mention of taking him back to the home, but he could've frozen to death if I hadn't been placed for a time such as that one.

Once I had to clear out a restroom because of drug users and homeless individuals camping out, and one particular regular decided to give me some attitude. Clearly, I was irritating him because, at one point, he took the syringe held in his hand, which I presume was full of a mixture of black tar heroin and his own blood and pointed it right at me while I was about six feet from him. I popped the hood of my holster and started to pull my gun while we locked our eyes. I could see the wheels turning in his head as he thought about his next step. Choosing to cap his needle instead, he quickly moved out of the bathroom, only to smoke meth in the elevator next to the bathrooms. A Denver PD officer and I proceeded to arrest this man and take him in on charges of possession and resisting arrest. The next time I saw him was about 4 months later.

He was quietly reading a college textbook, but it looked like he had finally put on weight, clean clothes and taken a bath.

All three situations had different outcomes but think about what would've happened if I didn't have the mindset I have. How easy would it have been for me to just force the first guy to move so he didn't loiter? Or let the second one walk out into the cold, active snow. Or even yet quickly drawing and ending the life of the last one. Thinking over the years that I've worked in security, I can safely say God has put me in many situations where I was used to provide counseling, food, or even a ride, especially when I could've just as easily enforced the rules, issued citations, called local PD, or just pushed people away from a client's property. I can't help but think it's because of my love for God that I go out of my way to show mercy when I can. Even so, it raises an interesting question: what good does it do to carry weapons around if I don't have the moral character to use them appropriately?

It's why the story from earlier has such a profound meaning. Any person can carry a weapon of war, but without the proper knowledge of God's expectations for the world, who cares? Me carrying a weapon is meaningless if I don't know what it means to be both merciful and just, which is a core concept that God displays over and over and over again throughout all of scripture. My willingness to work with people to help them through situations, I think, is driven by my desire to understand God's commands and a want to know what He thinks of all circumstances. I know there will be those who'll make the claim of not needing God to be moral, but I argue an atheist then has to justify whose morality they'll live by. If God doesn't get to set morality, then there's no standard for morality. After all, to a serial rapist, how dare anyone tell them not to be "true" to themselves. Same can be said of a nudist or a racist.

This I think is the point of the story: it's the spiritual leaders, those who help guide others into living right, that are the true protectors. With these people, any nation will rise to success or fall to its doom. I think most people don't realize the ramifications of what it means to be a spiritual leader, for the standard of their life is much higher than that of the normal person. As clearly indicated in Numbers 18:32, "**Moreover, because you will have set aside from it its best parts, you will not be committing any sin because of it; for <u>you are not to profane the holy things of the people of Isra'el, or you will die</u>**" (*emphasis added*). This is why I think James gives the warning he does in the 3rd chapter of his letter. By the leader's example people will either follow God closely or turn around and perish because of rejecting Him. Hence the warning Hosea gives the people in his book: "**My

people are destroyed for want of knowledge. Because you rejected knowledge, I will also reject you as *cohen* **for me. Because you forgot the** *Torah* **of your God, I will also forget your children**" (*Hosea 4:6*). Then there's the rebellion of Korra in Numbers 16 where he taught the people tolerance and pride. In doing such he caused the people to desire the return to slavery. Unfortunately, these kinds of teachings have infected many churches and synagogues like a deadly virus, leading them all into disastrous situations, and causing many to move even further and further away from God.

    So, what can be done to prevent the spiritual deaths of thousands? Seek to understand God's Face and understand that there's no difference between worship and work. This is why I guard places: I consider it an act of worship. I'm not doing it for whichever agency's uniform I wear, I do it to watch over and protect God's people. He'll make sure I am where I need to be to help whomever needs it. You also need to not just read the Bible but actively try and live by it. You need to let His Words change you from the inside out. I would suggest that you start reading Genesis 1:1 and don't stop until Revelation 22:21, then do it again, and again. Ultimately, knowing how to fight physically means nothing when fighting in a spiritual war.

XII. How Much Do I Believe?

"Throughout the period for which he has consecrated himself to *ADONAI*, he is not to approach a corpse. He is not to make himself unclean for his father, mother, brother or sister when they die, since his consecration to God is on his head. Throughout the time of his being a *nazir* he is holy for *ADONAI*"
-Numbers 6:6-8

I struggled to understand Numbers 6:6-8 for a long time. I couldn't understand why God would encourage family unity, repeatedly show why being a family unit is a good thing with lots of benefits, but then, while under a Nazir Vow, I was not allowed to attend the funeral of anyone. I'm glad and blessed that not a single member of my family died while I was under my vow, because I honestly think if one had, I may have ended up resenting God for forbidding me from going to their funeral. Given the knowledge I have now, I understand the difficulty behind this Law, and I would also, without hesitation, follow through on His rule. The rest of my family may become angry with me, but I no longer care.

What would I be willing to give up for my belief in God? I think most of us would agree to simple things like a little bit of time, a bit of money or old clothes, maybe a lifestyle for those who are getting really serious with their walk. What about social status or physical comfort… a loved one maybe? I bet most people cringed at the thought of giving up a family member or immediately went to the story of Abraham and Isaac. While Abraham was willing to give up Isaac (the promised son), Abraham did actually give up Ishmael, and he "**…became very distressed over this matter of his son**" (*Genesis 21:11*). Think of it this way, Abraham was willing to give up his whole future lineage for God.

      Plenty of others throughout all of Scripture have been put into similar positions, of choosing whether they'll fulfill their duty as a parent or not, or if they'll seek God fully or not. Hannah gave up Samuel in the first chapter of 1st Samuel. She prayed relentlessly until she conceived Samuel, but once he was weaned off breast milk, Hannah gave him up without hesitation. Ruth gave up her home country and people. Isaiah walked around naked to proselytize the people. Ezekiel laid on each of his sides for a number of days and cooked his food over dung. Jeremiah was beaten for his preaching and thrown into an empty cistern. Daniel was thrown into a den full of lions. Paul was beaten and lied about repeatedly and eventually beheaded for his troubles. Paul is still lied about, misunderstood and misquoted to this day. 10 of Yeshua's original 12 disciples were executed in varying ways, like crucifixion, hanging, being flayed open, beheading, and more. John the Baptist's head was placed on a silver platter and presented as a gift to the king's daughter. Lot was willing to give up two of his virgin daughters to spare two of God's angels from being raped by the town's men. Noah gave up the world as he knew it. Even in modern times, God's children have been beaten, raped, jailed, mutilated and executed just for existing. Some converts have even given up their family ties just because they choose to follow the God of Israel... Noticing a pattern yet?

Following God will not always be easy or fun, and sometimes life altering choices will be made. The next question should be obvious, *why would a God who wants unity cause division?* Simplest answer: "**You are to have no other gods before me**" (*Exodus 20:3*). God is very serious about this; unfortunately, we're stupid and can make almost anything into a false god. False gods like sex, power, ego, sports, wealth, and even social or familial status—pretty much anything that takes our eyes off of The Creator and keeps them on the creation. This is what Peter had to learn the hard way when he walked on the water with the Messiah, as recounted in Matthew 14:22-33. To put it simply, God wants people who want Him back, not people who give only lip service, "**[b]ecause these people** approach [Him] with empty words, and the honor they bestow on [Him] is mere lip-service; while in fact they have distanced their hearts from [Him], and their 'fear of [Him]' is just a *mitzvah* of human origin" (*Isaiah 29:13*).

Each of the people I listed willingly gave up something of actual value to God. *But then isn't God a hypocrite if He is not willing to do the same to prove His love for us?* If He is not willing to do the same, then yes, except He already has, "**For God so loved the world that he gave his only and unique Son, so that everyone who trusts in him may have eternal life, instead of being utterly destroyed. For God did not send the Son into the world to judge the world, but rather so that through him, the world might be saved**" (*John 3:16-17*). He didn't send His own flesh down to die in our place just so we could give Him lip service or so we could check Him off on a weekly to-do list. He sent His Son to be our stand in, just like God sent the ram as a stand in for Issac (Genesis 22:9-18). Even then, God also said that He was going to make a human sacrifice, and that this act would please Him while making many people righteous (Isaiah 53:10-12). As Zechariah 3:9 points out, this event would take place on a single day. Yeshua was lied about, beaten, ridiculed, stripped naked, and eventually led to a cross meant for Barabbas—a cross where He eventually died in the place of not only Barabbas but all of humanity as well. All of which pleased God. Not to watch His Own Son get treated in such a horrendous manner, but to provide a way for undeserving people to come back to Him, just like the undeserving people in Exodus. Perfectly shown in what God told Ezekiel, for God takes "**...no pleasure in having the wicked person die, but in having the wicked person turn from his way and live.** So repent! Turn from your evil ways! For why should you die, house of Isra'el?" (*Ezekiel 33:11, emphasis added*).

God doesn't want to separate families through the Messiah! Correct, God doesn't get pleasure from separating families, but that doesn't mean He won't do it for the greater good. Remember the Messiah, Himself, said "**I have come to set fire to the earth! And how I wish it were already kindled! I have an immersion to undergo — how pressured I feel till it's over! Do you think that I have come to bring peace in the Land? Not peace, I tell you, but division! For from now on, a household of five will be divided, three against two, two against three. Father will be divided against son and son against father, mother against daughter and daughter against mother, mother-in-law against her daughter-in-law and daughter-in-law against mother-in-law**" (*Luke 12:49-53, emphasis added*). Yeshua, Himself, whipped people and chased them from the Temple grounds (Matthew 21:12-13, Mark 11:15-18, and John 2:14-17). He ignored His own mother and siblings when they wanted to speak with Him (Matthew 12:46-50, and Mark 3:31-35), basically stating those who **do** His Father's will are His family. Literally curses a tree with death after He checks it for fruit (Matthew 21:18-22, and Mark 11:12-24). In John 6:22-71 we come across the aftereffects of Jesus feeding the multitudes with five loaves of bread and two fish. Pay attention to two things Yeshua himself says, "**Yes, indeed! I tell you, <u>you're not looking for me because you saw miraculous signs, but because you ate the bread and had all you wanted!</u>**" and "**But the bread that comes down from heaven is such that a person may eat it and not die. <u>I am the living bread that has come down from heaven; if anyone eats this bread, he will live forever</u>**" (*John 6:26, 50-51a, emphasis added*). He says this to a bunch of dietary conscious Jews who were shocked by the thought of eating a person's flesh. In verse 66 we find out that "**<u>many of his *talmidim* turned back and no longer traveled around with him</u>**" (*John 6:66, emphasis added*). Then, when we get to the Book of Revelation, chapters 2 and 3 are dedicated to seven different groups of believers. Five of the seven groups are told that they're messing up and need to turn back, lest He, Himself (Yeshua), snuff out their menorah and cast them away from Him. The last two groups, on the other hand, are told to keep on doing what they're doing. Clearly the Messiah has no problems in pushing away Fairweather followers.

Deuteronomy teaches two things about God choosing to separate families. One aspect is it's a curse for not fully following Him, as indicated in chapter 28 verses 15-69. The other aspect is God testing our hearts to see if we'll follow Him fully or not, because **"If your brother the son of your mother, or your son, or your daughter, or your wife whom you love, or your friend who means as much to you as yourself, secretly tries to entice you to go and serve other gods, which you haven't known, neither you nor your ancestors — gods of the peoples surrounding you, whether near or far away from you, anywhere in the world — you are not to consent, and you are not to listen to him; and you must not pity him or spare him; and you may not conceal him. <u>Rather, you must kill him!</u> Your own hand must be the first one on him in putting him to death, and afterwards the hands of all the people"** (*Deuteronomy 13:7-10, emphasis added*). God clearly doesn't want followers who are only there when times are good, which is why Abraham was so blessed. He gave up one child and was willing to give up the actual child of promise. King Saul lost his kingdom and had most of his bloodline snuffed out because he wouldn't follow God wholeheartedly.

Once saved, always saved. I am washed in the Blood of Messiah. His blood is strong enough to wipe away all sins, past, present and future, but this **DOES NOT** mean we have a free pass to continue living sinfully. Doing so would be putting Yeshua back on the cross over and over again (*Hebrews 6:1-8*), thus making a mockery of what He did. The Messiah repeatedly tells people to go forth and sin no more, including the 5 churches in Revelation 2 & 3. Yeshua also tells us that we can't be forgiven if we don't forgive each other. In the parable of the four seeds, two died out because of being either strangled by the cares of the world or from having no deep roots of faith (*Matthew 13:3-12, Mark 4:3-20, Luke 8:5-15*). Then there's all the warnings given by the prophet Ezekiel, the ones where he preaches on turning from wickedness. If a person chooses to live rightly, then ALL of their past wickedness will be forgotten. Similarly, if a person chooses to live contrary to God's way, then ALL of their past righteousness will be forgotten (*Ezekiel 3:10-21, 18:21-32, 33:12-20*). Since we know that Yeshua is the Passover lamb, there's a very simple detail about the first Passover which needs to be pointed out. Once Moses had received the instructions from God, the leaders were instructed to "**[t]ake a bunch of hyssop leaves and dip it in** the blood which is in the basin, and smear it on the two sides and top of the door-frame. Then, **none of you is to go out the door of his house until morning.** For *ADONAI* will pass through to kill the Egyptians; but when he sees the blood on the top and on the two sides, *ADONAI* will pass over the door and will not allow the Slaughterer to enter your houses and kill you'"** (*Exodus 12:22-23, emphasis added*). We're ordered to stay inside of the house until after the judgment has passed, which is why the Messiah repeatedly warns about disobeying God's commands. We cannot lose our salvation once we've been washed, but we can choose to give it up by continuing to live in disobedience. Since the great and terrible day (the Judgment), has not come and passed over us yet.

Now when I look at Numbers 6:6-8, I realize that these verses are not about God being punitive or arbitrary, it's about God not wanting a shallow follower. When I took the vow, I had to be all in, no compromises. No vow should ever be taken lightly, regardless of the vow, because you don't want to "...**let your words make you guilty, and don't tell the temple official that you made the vow by mistake. Why give God reason to be angry at what you say and destroy what you have accomplished?**" (*Ecclesiastes 5:5, emphasis added*). A concept I wish I fully understood before I got married. Oh well, another hard knock lesson for me. Thank God His mercy is new every day, because without it, I'd be screwed.

How do I stop sinning? Left to our own devices, we can't: hence our need for God. We <u>need</u> to use His strength, and, when we're struggling, push even deeper into Him. For me personally, I have to make a point of spending time with God by either reading His word, praying, fasting and/or worshiping Him. When temptation becomes hard to resist, and it does become hard at times, you need to press more urgently into God. You have to speak His word over yourself again and again and again, until the temptation stops. Case in point, a little while ago, I was sitting with my sister and mother at her kitchen table. I don't know what was in the air that morning, but I became overly angry at them both. It's not like my sister could help it, she's severely disabled, and my mother was trying to help her. Blowing up on them would've caused a needless argument between my mother and I, which would've been the easiest thing to do. Instead, I chose to separate myself quietly and chant "Your Grace is sufficient." I did this over and over again until my anger subsided. Loving God is a choice that I've already decided for myself everyday (*Deuteronomy 30, Joshua 24:14-15, Ecclesiastes 12:13-14*). *Easier said than done*, I agree. Choosing self-control is never easy; however, the alternative is not worth giving up the war for my soul.

About the Author

Zachary James grew up in Denver, Colorado of the United States. He came to know the real God at age 20, and since then he's walked with Him in the ups and downs of life. During his long career as a security guard, he's worked both Federal and private, armed and unarmed. He's even successfully put himself through a Police Academy in 2017, and eventually received his associate's in law enforcement in 2018. His favorite hobbies include reading books and watching historical documentaries. While in High School, some of his English teachers noticed his raw talent for writing, but until now he's only used that gift for writing official reports. Now he wants to share with the world all the lessons he's learned about God in both a practical and real-life manner. His only goal is to help with the harvest by strengthening God's children.

Works Cited

Bary, Rifqa. *Hiding in the Light: Why I Risked Everything to Leave Islam and Follow Jesus.* Crown Publishing Group, 2016.

Cahn, Jonathan. *The Oracle: The Jubilean Mysteries Unveiled.* Lake Mary, Charisma House, 2019.

Cosper, Mike. *Promised Land.* February 2024. 6 vols. *Spotify*, Christianity Today. PodCast.

Dershowitz, Alan. *The Case for Israel.* Wiley, 2003.

Fee, Gordon D., and Douglas Stuart. *How to Read the Bible for All Its Worth: Fourth Edition.* Zondervan, 2014.

Feuer, Avrohom Chaim, and Avie Gold, translators. *Complete Tishah b'Av service.* Brooklyn, Mesorah Publications, 1991.

Fruchtenbaum, Arnold G. *Yeshua: The Life of the Messiah from a Messianic Jewish Perspective.* San Antonio, Ariel Ministries, 2017.

Fu, Bob, and Nancy French. *God's Double Agent: The True Story of a Chinese Christian's Fight for Freedom.* Baker Publishing Group, 2014.

Gersh, Rabbi Akiva. *75 Hebrew Words You Need to Understand the Bible: In Honor of*

Israel At 75. Edited by Rabbi Elie Mischel, Israel365, 2023.

Kirzner, Yitzchok, and Lisa Aiken. *The Art of Jewish Prayer*. Jason Aronson, 1991.

Kulp, Joshua. *English Explanation of Mishnah Nazir*. 1997. *https://www.sefaria.org/*, Learn Conservative Yeshiva, https://www.sefaria.org/English_Explanation_of_Mishnah_Nazir%2C_Introduction.1?lang=bi&with=About&lang2=en. Accessed 9 April 2024.

Kushner, Aviya. *The Grammar of God: A Journey Into the Words and Worlds of the Bible*. Spiegel & Grau, 2015.

Lewis, C. S. *The C. S. Lewis Signature Classics: An Anthology of 8 C. S. Lewis Titles: Mere Christianity, The Screwtape Letters, Miracles, The Great Divorce, The Problem of Pain, A Grief Observed, The Abolition of Man, and The Four Loves*. HarperCollins, 2017.

McDowell, Josh, and Sean McDowell. *More Than a Carpenter*. Tyndale House Publishers, Incorporated, 2009.

Messianic Jewish Family Bible Society. *Messianic Jewish Family Bible: Tree of Life Version*. Messianic Jewish Family Bible, 2018.

Metaxas, Eric, director. *Letter to the American Church*. Metaxas Media, 2024.

Nachshoni, Yehuda. *Studies in the Weekly Parashah*. Translated by Raphael Blumberg and Yaakov Petroff, vol. IV: Bamidbar, Brooklyn, Mesorah Publications Ltd., 1989.

Naḥmanides. *Commentary on the Torah*. Edited by Charles Ber Chavel, translated by Charles Ber Chavel, Shilo Publishing House, 1971.

Prager, Dennis, and Joseph Telushkin. *Why the Jews? The Reason for Antisemitism*. Touchstone, 2003.

Qureshi, Nabeel. *Seeking Allah, Finding Jesus: A Devout Muslim Encounters Christianity*. Zondervan, 2018.

Roeh Israel. *Erev Shabbat Service - Yeshua Our Asham*. 30 August 2024. *Youtube*, https://www.youtube.com/watch?v=pfR4e5n9QjM. Accessed 30 August 2024.

Rubin, Rabbi Barry. *The Complete Jewish Study Bible: Insights for Jews & Christians: Illuminating the Jewishness of God's Word*. Edited by Rabbi Barry Rubin, translated by David H. Stern, Hendrickson Bibles, 2016.

Stern, David H. *Complete Jewish Bible Flexisoft*. Translated by David H. Stern, Clarksville, Messianic Jewish Publishers, 2017.

Stern, David H. *Restoring the Jewishness of the Gospel: A Message to Christians*. 3rd ed., Clarksville, Messianic Jewish Publishers, 2010.

Stone, Perry. *Breaking the Jewish Code*. Charisma House, 2009.

Strobel, Lee. *The Case for Christ: A Journalist's Personal Investigation of the Evidence for Jesus*. Zondervan, 2016.

Talmidi Israelite Community. "Torah, not Talmud – Living God's Way." *World Fellowship of Followers of the Way*, https://talmidi.co.il/articles-on-talmidaism/torah-not-talmud-living-gods-way/. Accessed 4 May 2024.

Weisz, Rabbi Tuly, editor. *The Israel Bible: The Only Hebrew Bible Highlighting the Land and the People of Israel*. 2nd ed., Israel365, 2021.

Wilson, Marvin R. *Our Father Abraham: Jewish Roots of the Christian Faith*. Eerdmans Publishing Company, 1989.

Yousef, Mosab Hassan, and Ron Brackin. *Son of Hamas*. SaltRiver, 2011.

Zlotowitz, Meir, and Avie Gold, editors. *The Complete ArtScroll Machzor Yom Kippur*. Translated by Nosson Scherman, 22nd ed., Brooklyn, Mesorah Publications, Ltd., 1986.

www.ingramcontent.com/pod-product-compliance
Lightning Source LLC
Chambersburg PA
CBHW020944090426
42736CB00010B/1261